Animals in Their Habitats

Forest Animals

Francine Galko

Heinemann Library
Chicago, Illinois

© 2003 Heinemann Library
Published by Heinemann Library,
an imprint of Capstone Global Library, LLC.,
Chicago, Illinois
Customer Service 888-454-2279
Visit our website at www.heinemannlibrary.com

Designed by Ginkgo Creative
Printed in the United States of America in Eau Claire, Wisconsin.
092013 007714R

Library of Congress Cataloging-in-Publication Data

Galko, Francine.
    Forest animals / Francine Galko.
        p. cm. — (Animals in their habitats)
Includes bibliographical references (p.   ).
Summary: Explores the animals whose habitat is the forest.
    ISBN 1-40340-179-9 (HB), 978-1-4034-0179-3 (HB), 1-4034-0436-4 (Pbk.), 978-1-4034-0436-7 (Pbk.)
    1. Forest animals—Juvenile literature. [1. Forest animals.] I.Title.
    QL112 .G245 2002
    591.73—dc21

                                    2001007655

Acknowledgments
The author and publishers are grateful to the following for permission to reproduce copyright material:
Cover photograph by J.D. Taylor/Bruce Coleman Inc.
pp. 4, 12, 21 Dwight Kuhn; p. 5 Russell A. Mittermeir/Bruce Coleman Inc.; p. 6 Julie Eggers/Bruce Coleman Inc.; p. 7 Barbara Williams/Bruce Coleman Inc.; p. 8 Tom Brakefield/Bruce Coleman Inc.; pp. 9, 23 Joe McDonald/Bruce Coleman Inc.; p. 10 W. Patton/OSF/Animals Animals; p. 11 Joe McDonald/Animals Animals; p. 13 E. R. Degginger/Bruce Coleman Inc.; p. 14 John Shaw/Bruce Coleman Inc.; p. 15 David Madison/Bruce Coleman Inc.; p. 16 J. D. Taylor/Bruce Coleman Inc.; p. 17 Richard Day/Animals Animals; p. 18 Breck P. Kent/Animals Animals; pp. 19, 24, 29 Zig Leszczynski/Animals Animals; p. 20 Gerard Fuehrer/Visuals Unlimited; p. 22 Richard Alan Wood/Animals Animals; p. 25 Frans Lanting/Minden Pictures; p. 26 Carol McDonald/Bruce Coleman Inc.; p. 27 C. W. Schwartz/Animals Animals; p. 28 Erwin and Peggy Bauer/Bruce Coleman Inc.Every effort has been made to contact copyright holders of any material reproduced in this book. Any omissions will be rectified in subsequent printings if notice is given to the publisher.

Some words are shown in bold, **like this.** You can find out what they mean by looking in the glossary.

To learn more about the marten on the cover, turn to page 16.

Contents

What is a Forest?

A forest is a kind of **habitat.** It is a place where many trees grow side by side. In a **deciduous** forest, the trees lose all their leaves just before winter.

The trees in a **coniferous** forest keep their leaves all year. These forests are sometimes called **evergreen** forests.

Where are Forests?

Forests are all over the world. Rain forests grow in warm places where the seasons change very little during the year. Rain forests get lots of rain.

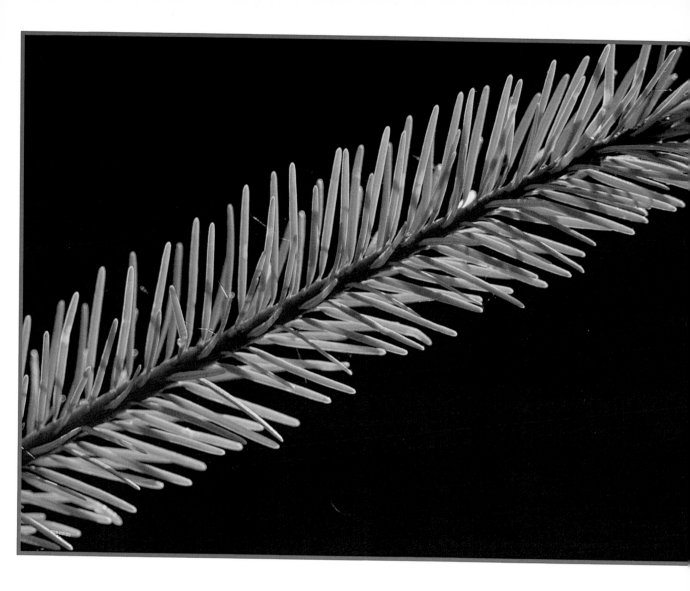

In cold places, some forests have trees with leaves that look like needles. Different kinds of forests grow in different parts of the world.

 # Forest Homes

Forests have many homes for animals. Porcupines live on the forest floor. They walk slowly, but they are fast when they climb trees. Porcupines eat tree bark and branches.

Great horned owls often sit in trees. They rest during the day. At night, they hunt for food.

Living Underground

Many animals **burrow** under the ground and make a home there. Rabbits live in dens under the forest floor.

Badgers are very good at digging holes in the ground. They live underground and usually come out at night to look for food.

Living on the Forest Floor

Leaves on the forest floor form **leaf litter.**
Pill bugs and other small animals live in
the leaf litter. Unlike real bugs, pill bugs
breathe through **gills.**

12

Earthworms also live on the forest floor.
They move through the soil and leaves.
Earthworms break the soil into pieces and
make it easy for plants to grow.

Living in the Tree Branches

Ocelots are forest cats. They often sleep in the tree branches during the day. At night, they wake up and hunt for food.

Monarch butterflies do not live in forests all year. They **migrate** to warm forests in the winter. They spend their winters in forest trees.

Living in the Tree Trunk

Some animals make their homes inside tree trunks. **Martens** make their homes in **hollow** tree trunks. They also climb the tree branches to hunt squirrels.

Woodpeckers can climb around on trees and make holes in tree trunks. They make a nest in one hole. Then they lay eggs inside.

Finding Food in the Forest

Forests have many plants and small animals to eat. Gray squirrels eat seeds and nuts in the forest. Sometimes, squirrels eat eggs, young birds, or insects.

Brown skinks eat insects and spiders. They have clear eyelids, so they can see even with their eyes closed! This helps them find food in the dirt without getting dirt in their eyes.

# Forest Predators

Many forest animals are **predators**. They hunt other animals in the forest. Cooper's hawks have strong **talons** and wings. Their talons help them grab and hold on to tree branches.

20

Stoats are good hunters. They have sharp, pointed teeth. Stoats usually hunt mice. But they will even hunt rabbits and other animals larger than they are.

 # Traveling in a Forest

Flying squirrels don't really fly. They jump from branch to branch. The skin between their arms and legs is like a blanket that helps them float through the air. They use their tail to steer.

Bats are not birds, but they can fly. At night, little brown bats hunt insects. They eat moths, mosquitoes, and flies.

Hiding in a Forest

Camouflage is one way to hide from **predators.** The gray tree frog's skin looks like tree bark. This camouflage hides the frog from predators.

Katydids are **insects** that look like leaves. It's hard to find them in the forest. They hide in the trees.

Forest Babies

Forests have many places for animals to have babies. Deer mice have their babies in an underground nest. They have as many as nine baby mice at one time.

Baby American woodcocks hatch in a nest on the forest floor. If a **predator** is near, the babies freeze, or hold very still. Woodcocks are hard to see because they are **camouflaged.**

 # Protecting Forest Animals

Sometimes people cut down all the trees in a forest. We use the wood to make homes and paper. We build roads and buildings where trees used to grow. Forest animals lose their homes when we cut down too many trees.

If we recycle paper, we don't have to cut down so many trees. People should build a long road around a forest, not a short road through the forest. Then the rabbits, owls, and woodpeckers can keep their homes.

 Glossary

burrow to dig under the ground

camouflage way an animal hides itself

coniferous type of tree that has leaves shaped like needles and that stays green all year

deciduous type of tree that loses its leaves in fall and winter

evergreen type of tree that keeps its leaves and is green all year

hollow empty inside

habitat place where an animal lives

insect small animal with six legs

leaf litter leaves and dirt on the forest floor

marten animal that looks like a **stoat,** but is bigger

migrate move to another place when the seasons change

predator animal that hunts and eats other animals

prey animal that is hunted and eaten by another animal

soil dirt that is full of nutrients and good for plants to grow in

stoat a type of weasel, a long thin animal. It is not much longer than this book and weighs about as much as this book.

talon claws on a bird

More Books to Read

Arnosky, Jim. *Crinkleroot's Guide to Knowing Animal Habitats.* New York: Aladdin Picture Books, 1998.

Eugene, Tony. *Hide and Seek.* Washington, D.C. National Geographic Society, 1999.

Fowler, Allan. *Our Living Forests.* Danbury, Conn.: Children's Press, 1999.

Krupinski, Loretta. *Into the Woods: A Woodland Scrapbook.* New York: HarperCollins Children's Books, 1997.

Robbins, Ken. *Autumn Leaves.* New York: Scholastic Trade. 1998.

Index